THE BOOK BOOK

A Journey into Bookmaking

Sophie Benini Pietromarchi

TARA BOOKS

BOOKS ARE
LIKE HOUSES

Curiosity always makes me want to open
doors. I've always thought that the most
mysterious doors are the covers of books.
"How's that?" I hear you ask. Well, to
start with they open up in the same
way and they both protect their
insides. When they open, you
can see a whole other
world in there.

There's
something
about a door or
a book cover that
separates inside from
outside, that promises
to reveal secrets. Everything
about a cover or a door speaks
silently: the colour, the shape, the
decoration, the words written on it.
You're thinking, 'But in a book there's
no doorbell and nobody opens it from
the inside!' But still, there's something very
similar between a book and a house, and
sometimes entering a book is like entering
a house: you can smell the smells, notice
the dark corners and the light areas, the
moods of the person who lives in the
house, the things in there. Just like a
house, a book is a whole world –
like an egg perhaps – except
that an egg doesn't
have a door!

My love
of doors and
book covers has
led me into some of
the greatest adventures
of my life. I always loved
making play houses as a child,
and even as a grown up. I have
to say that my house is very similar
to a play house! I've discovered a
connection between play houses and
books: I started making books in the
same way as play houses are made. So
with little things found here and there,
I make up worlds and create books. Just
like you go around gathering treasures
to make your play house seem real, I
gather treasures to make my books real.
Of course, you can start to make a
book by simply writing a story, but
this time why not let yourself be
carried off, swept away, thrilled
by the things around you?

1

LOOKING INTO THE PAST

The first door on our trip opens... and shows us what kind of books were made in the past.

People then must have felt a great need to write. So they first invented writing, and wrote on all sorts of things: stones, clay, bone, wood, papyrus leaves, palm leaves, animal skin, silk, paper, even sheets made from elephants' feet. The first books were probably not like the books we know, they were more like long rolls of painted paper, called scrolls. Printing was only invented in the 15th century, so before that, each book was written and coloured by hand, just as we're going to do.

Ancient scroll books made of palm leaves

Looking to the past is a great way to discover new ideas. You get to know and love certain kinds of books — then you try to make one of your own. It's like when we make play houses, we think of houses that were made in the past or houses in stories, like the Three Little Pigs' house.

TREASURE HUNT

Now the trip calls for something very important: learning to turn the things you love into treasure. Start by collecting all the things you like. Gather all the books you've ever liked. You need to create your personal treasure library – your favourite illustrated books for instance, or useful books like encyclopaedias, which can be very handy when you forget what a pig's snout looks like.

Shall we make a book? If you've got even an inkling of an idea write it down now, and go on to the chapter titled *Writing a Story* (pg 62).

But I like to do it another way. I start by gathering all the things I think I'll need in a big basket in my mind. If you're the same, follow me and we'll ramble along on a treasure hunt.

But before we start our hunt, we need to follow one rule, an extremely strict rule:

There are no rules!

Feel free to pick up whatever catches your fancy; go about looking for things like an explorer in a new country. As you go along, a strange thing will start to happen. The treasure you're gathering will start falling into place in your mind, like the pieces of a jigsaw puzzle. It will begin to make sense, create a picture, and from this you will get the idea for your book.

The things we gather can turn into all sorts of other things. To understand how, stop and look carefully at what you've picked up. Look at its shape, feel its surface, see if you can look through it − is it turning into something else?

2.1

LOOK INSIDE YOUR PENCIL CASE

We're not going very far, we're going to start by looking inside your **school pencil case.**

You'll realise that you can do things you never imagined with the things you use every day. The people you want to put in your book will just pop out without your even realising it – but you do need to use all your powers of make believe, and learn to work well with the tools you have. So open up that basket in your mind and let's go...

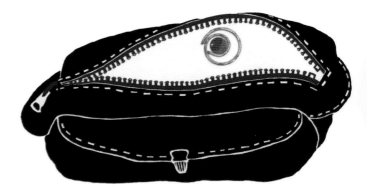

The pencil can be useful for a whole lot of things. When you sharpen it, it works miracles.

The dust from the pencil can be used to show real dust. Collect it on a piece of paper, put glue all over the surface to be dusted, then tip the dust onto it.

Pencil dust can be smeared onto a page to show smoke from a steam engine or a factory chimney.

The **wood shavings** that fall to
your feet when you sharpen a pencil
can become...

cocks' crests...

insect wings...

or a king's crown.

They're also good for making a ballerina's dress, a bird's feathers, wooden floors, fairies and sunrays. What else can you come up with?

I collect pencil shavings, especially those with different coloured edges, and glue them on carefully.

The **ballpoint pen** has its own quick, sharp way of writing, and leaves threads of ink on the paper. Nothing scribbles better than a ballpoint pen.

Look what masterpieces you can come up with: I actually saw spiders hanging from the threads... that's how real they seem.

The ballpoint pen is also
very good at drawing
hair...

telephone wires...

or a dog's coat.

The **fountain pen** makes beautiful splodges, even if you don't want them.

I drop a **blob of ink**
on a sheet of paper and fold it. When I open the sheet again, the blob's turned into a great pattern.

I cut these patterns out, glue them carefully onto a clean page and make up a story.

Blots? Mistakes? Not to worry, mistakes can be good sometimes. The weirdest shapes – and stories – can come out of blots.

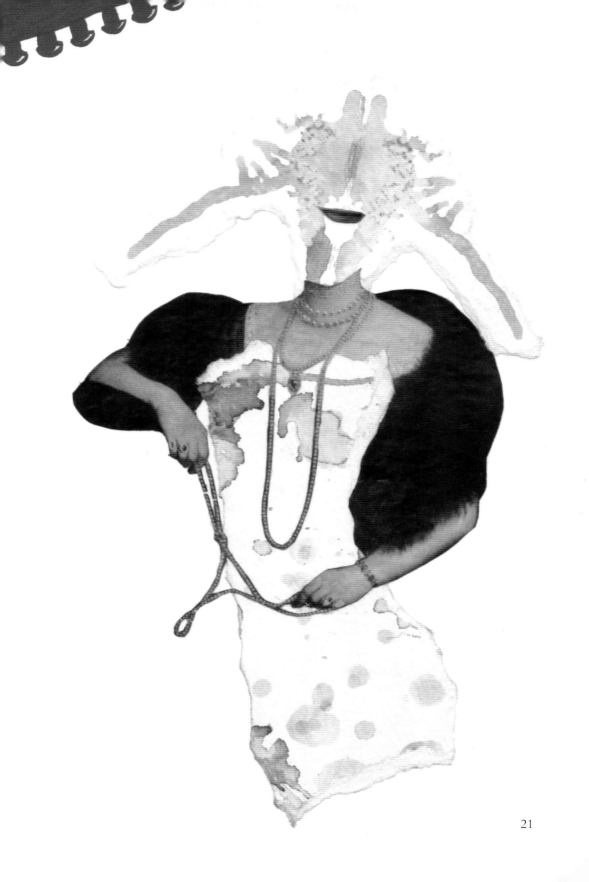

The eraser is not just there to rub things out, it can make light.

I colour a whole page in pencil, smear it around with my finger,

then I draw waves, rain, light... all with an eraser.

22

The paper clip:

I make animals by gluing together paper clips.

The colours on these clips look like a zebra and a tiger.

The highlighter allows light to shine out of
the darkness. I first draw the light, using
the highlighter, keeping in mind
where it's going to come from –
a streetlight? Car headlights?
A spaceship?
Then I colour the
background black.

Tipp-ex or white correction fluid knows about light too. It can make an ogre's skin. Or create snow. I first paint the background and then use Tipp-ex, making dots for the snow and squiggles for the skin.

The paintbrush skis in many ways. For very different effects, try it with different amounts of water.

Used like a hammer, it forms spectacular skies.
With a very dry brush, I do bristly bears'
coats or if the brush is really horrible,
I cut it up and glue it in as
a witch's broom.

Vinyl glue (Fevicol) is useful for making drops of rain. I take a thick sheet of tracing paper and paint it with acrylic paint. Then I drip drops of vinyl glue on it, let them dry and rip them off the paper.

A glue stick is not only useful for gluing but also for decorating. I rub a glue stick on a piece of coloured paper from a magazine, and also over my own drawing. It colours my work like plaster on a faded wall.

Sticky tape is not just for holding things together. You can make a TV screen with transparent tape.★

(★This is Carlo Alvarez's idea, thanks!)

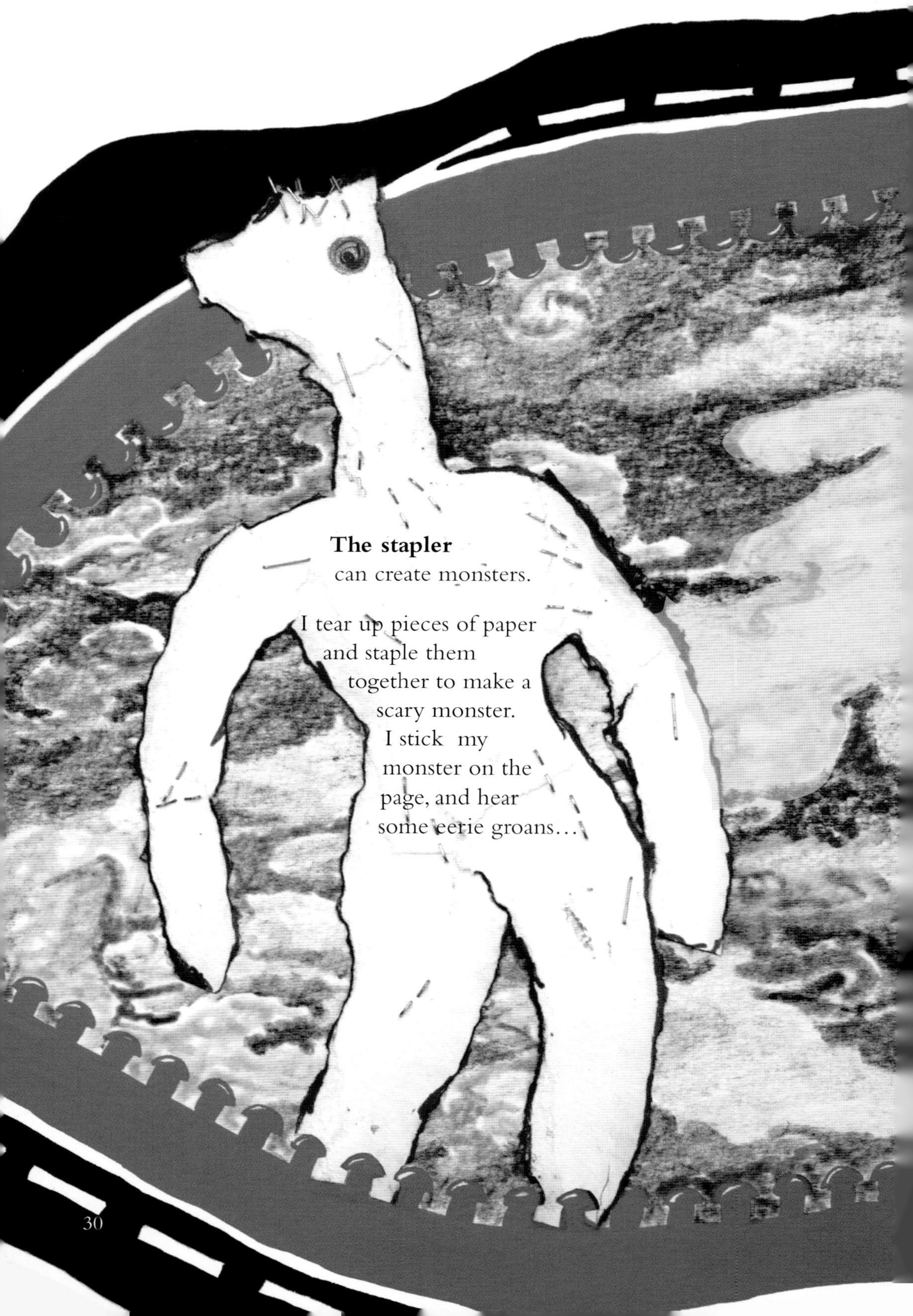

The stapler
can create monsters.

I tear up pieces of paper
and staple them
   together to make a
   scary monster.
   I stick my
   monster on the
   page, and hear
   some eerie groans…

Felt pens that don't work well make lovely faded colours. Felt pens that do work are good for painting on metallic things, and stand out against other colours.

Coloured pencils have the same qualities as crayons, and make great multi-coloured shavings and dust.

The lines they leave are soft and strong – good for things you don't want looking too obvious.

34

Chalks make shadows.
They make stunning skies
and foggy woods too.

They mix very well together, and if you keep rubbing and turning
with your finger, you'll see what great effects you get. But they have
to be fixed with varnish or spray, or they will smear.

Watercolours are beautiful, if you learn how to use them well. Put clean water on paper with a brush, dilute your chosen colour with water, and brush it on. Turn the paper over and over to chase the colour here and there. You can make backgrounds that quiver like water.

Poster paint has to be applied with a balance of colour and water, using little strokes. If the surface area is large, use a large brush to create the effect of Japanese prints. It's also nice to write your text on a splash of poster paint, it makes your book look elegant.

Oil paints can make marbled paper (to find out more, go to pg 61).

So you see, each thing in your pencil case has a different character and leads you a different way. It's fun to mix all these effects up too. For instance, you could do a lake with watercolours, fog using chalks, a hammock with a ballpoint pen – all in one picture.

Then you become a magician with your pencil case, showing off all its secrets.

2.2

GO INTO THE KITCHEN

Open the fridge!

An egg box has a great shape, especially for making book covers. Cut off the cones, stick them onto the cover, and colour them in. The egg box also makes a great front door.

Onion is good for decorating paper. Cut the bottom off the onion, dip it into diluted paint, and use it to make prints on paper. You can also use okra and other vegetables to make stamps. The Italian designer, Bruno Munari used this technique.

The Kitchen Cupboard

Rough string can bind books, become a tight-rope walkers rope, or create mazes. It's the most reliable thing in the kitchen. You stick it on with glue.

Boxes of cornflakes or biscuits make good book covers. They can also illustrate colourful cars or cities.

41

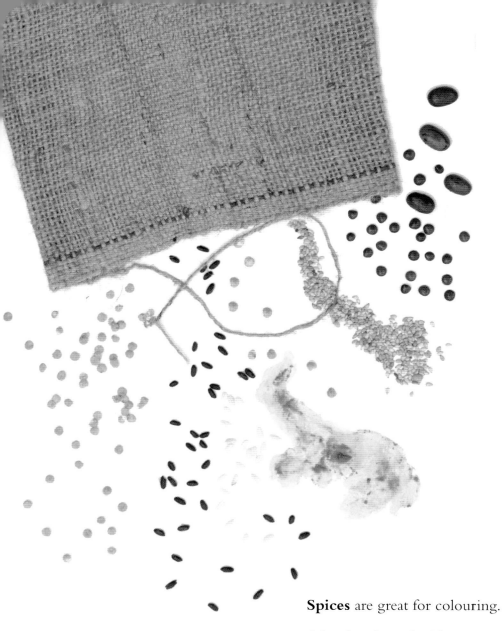

Spices are great for colouring.

A book coloured with **curry powder** and a bit of diluted glue is so bright and smells so good that I could almost eat it.

Then there's **saffron** and **cinnamon** — if you use them with glue they make endless deserts and rocky mountains.

Why not illustrate a recipe book with elephants made of **lentils?**

43

Lots of animals hide in
peas and beans.

I draw the animal in pencil, and
outline each part in a different colour.
Each colour will be a different dried bean.
I dip one side of a bean in glue, and paste it in
place, covering the area bean by bean. Finally, I brush
a layer of diluted glue over the finished animal.

This isn't the end, every kitchen has its own special items
– who knows what you'll find in yours and what you can
turn it into.

2.3

SCRAPS AROUND THE HOUSE

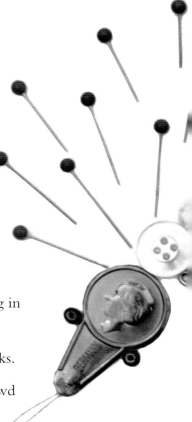

Buttons are pretty — they can be used on covers, as wheels, as a donkey's nose, as planets or as eyes shining in the dark.

Beads make beautiful clothes or handles for shiny forks.

Careful with **pins**, but blunt ones can turn into a crowd seen from the top of a skyscraper.

Safety pins can look more real than real insects.

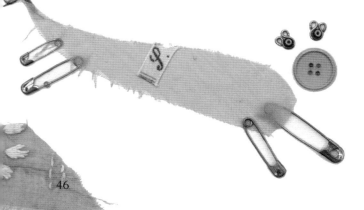

46

Don't the **pins** make this beaver look like a porcupine instead?

Ribbons and braids are great for building castles, decorating living rooms, creating glorious dresses or trimming books.

Coloured thread can be used to decorate your book, but can also become hair or cheerful-looking cobwebs.

Scraps of fabric? By now, you're an expert at reading stories in scraps of things. When you're working with scraps, think carefully of what exactly they could become – dragons' wings, pretty dresses, sofa covers…

In Your Cupboard

Leftover **decorations** from your birthday party can become kings' tunics, enchanted animals or rainbows to decorate your book with.

Old toys can become anything you want – an old puzzle can become a wooden floor, an old domino can be a building in the desert and an old wheel can be a mill.

How full is your imaginary basket now?

It's always good to save some used things such as **tickets, postcards, letters, exercise books, calendars** and **posters.**

Here you can find many different worlds, numbers and funny characters... use them to create your own characters or make paper monsters.

I often use letters cut from **newspapers** in my illustrations. I use foreign newspapers with letters that look like figures to decorate the covers of my books.

51

2.4

WANDERING AROUND

And now after so much wandering around the house, we're going out for a walk. We'll gather everything that the park, wood, road and beach have to offer.

Pebbles, feathers, leaves, seashells, snail shells, twigs, seeds... and much more.

Let the things you collect lead you on, and suddenly, you'll find they transform into the oddest things.

my sea

Here is my favourite game: I take an
object, and look at it over and over
– at the shape, the colour, the texture,
everything. Soon it begins to make me
think of something else, and that's how I
create my book. I start making the things
in my mind, using little objects, turning
them into a new form.

So the **red leaves** become flames,
a **piece of plastic** turns into a wolf's muzzle,
a **lentil** becomes an eye...

Watch out for my blue wolf!

2.5

PAPER

So have we collected enough? If you have more ideas, now is the time to write them down. Put your treasures in front of you and give your imagination a stir.

I want to add something important to your basket – I want to take you through the world of paper, because that's where the soul of a book hides itself. Paper is like the skin of a book.

There are different kinds of paper; you have to get to know them all: **gift paper, handmade paper, printed paper,** paper you make yourself.

Look closely at your paper. Can you see through it? Feel it, is it rough or smooth? Look how deep and beautiful its colour is.

Every piece of paper reminds you of something that has happened before – it is a memory. It could tell you of the people who made it or if it is from an old exercise book, it can even transport you straight back in time to the classrooms in your great-great-grandfather's school.

It might have come from China, from Japan, from India, from anywhere in the world, and you can make it travel even further. Each piece of paper is a great chance – you can actually give it a life. What kind of life depends on what kind of paper it is, what you can call its character – its pattern, colour and light, all these make each piece of paper different from every other. Feel it and look at it very closely. The longer you study it, the more ideas you'll find popping up. Any piece of paper will listen to you, and with the help of glue it can become whatever you want.

Thick paper is made up of many layers — like clouds, like a forest seen from above, like furry bear skin, like a rough tree trunk. It is so heavy that you can actually make it look like tar on a city road. Look, touch — it's coarse and you can't see through it. That's the texture of the paper. Think of all the rough, heavy things you know: like a huge overcoat, big boots... then think of the opposite, something delicate, like a fairy's hat.

What does **coloured paper** remind you of? It can be thick or thin, and sometimes the effect is like a scene on a city street where some things are clear and others hazy. Sometimes the paper looks like plastic. If you can see through the colours, that's great, you can use the papers in layers, like thin cloth, one on top of the other. That's called transparency. You can come up with a huge sky or windows for a building. See how fluttery paper can be good for making a butterfly's wings. It reminds me of the wrappers that covered sweets I used to eat when I was little.

Printed paper is useful for decorating houses, making clothes, creating a field, or making a road. It has so much character that it makes any shape stand out.

Some papers look like they're straight from outer space. You can use them for anything metallic and shiny, like cars, robots or to show a magic spell.

See-through, light and **plasticky** paper is fun to use for adding little touches to something you've already painted, to make a strip of light, for example. It feels very modern when you touch it; it seems to belong in a city.

So there you have it: colour, texture, transparency, layers, heaviness, lightness. Get carried away – does it look animal, vegetable, human?

What can you do with paper?

You can cut it, if you're interested in using only a part of it.

Tear it and it can become a meadow of flowers or a suit of armour.

Crumple it and it turns into a rhinoceros.

Paint over it, leaving only the bits that you like.

Decorating paper

Papier maché

1. Put some vinyl glue (Fevicol) in a bowl.

2. Stir in spoonfuls of water till the mixture becomes creamy and smooth.

3. Tear up pieces of coloured paper and dip them in the bowl.

4. Fish them out carefully, one by one, and put them in layers on any surface you choose, depending on the shape you want.

5. When it dries, papier maché becomes very hard. Then you can stick it on to things or make sculptures. Handles or book covers are great to make this way.

Cloth paper

You can make paper look like cloth by filling it with a regular pattern. To get this effect, make your own stamps with vegetables (see *Go into the kitchen*, pg 38). Paint any background onto a sheet of paper, then use your stamps on it. You can also create and use your own stencils by cutting shapes out from paper or cardboard.

Marbled paper

The Chinese and the Persians used to marble paper hundreds of years ago, and now we're going to imitate them.

1. Take a shallow dish wide enough to hold sheets of paper, and fill it with water.

2. Find a pair of rubber gloves and put them on. (I suspect the Persians didn't have quite the same materials).

3. Pour a spoonful of diluted oil paint into a cup. Use one cup for each colour.

4. Empty the contents of the cups into the shallow dish. With an old comb, draw patterns on the oil paint, which will float on top of the water.

5. Take a sheet of paper, dip it carefully into the dish and pull it out quickly. Marbled paper!

Marbled paper is lovely for making book covers. You can use bits of marbled paper for other things as well – to create landscapes, moody skies or even hair.

WRITING A STORY

Now that you have a storehouse of treasures and secrets, you can start writing – but this can be the hardest part. So how do you turn your treasures into a tale?

What if we don't write the stories, but just allow them to be written by us?

I believe that a book can write itself. You just have to be in the right mood, be open, and let your ideas fly out freely like butterflies... and wham! Just catch one when its least expecting it.

Being open this way is not easy, but I've got a solution that's practically magical, an invention of mine that almost never fails. I call it massaging your imagination, because you gently stroke and nudge your mind along.

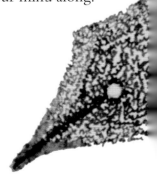

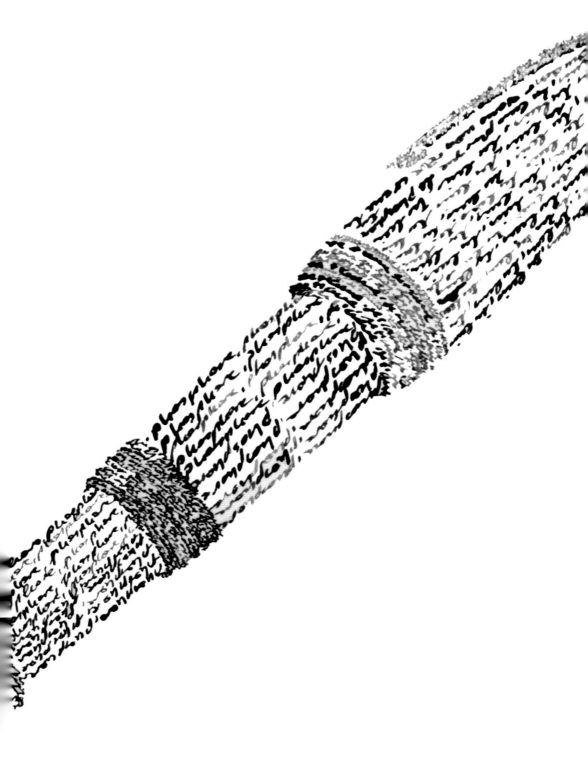

3.1

MASSAGING YOUR IMAGINATION

Write your answers on a
sheet of paper:

Your favourite word

The word you hate most

The word hardest to understand

An adult word

A scary word

A word that makes you fall asleep

A word that makes you dream

A magic word

A word you keep repeating

Everything you want, in three words

A weapon-word

A kind word

An old word

A word that sounds funny

Describe:

A fairy

A gift

A friend

A magic potion

A bizarre plant

Your suitcase

Something changing into something else

Imagine a country, describe:

A forest

A journey

A secret code

A trap

Something you have to overcome

Somebody who helps you

Your favourite number

Your favourite colour

Describe:

A maze

A place to hide

Your favourite prince

Your favourite princess

Your house

Your castle

Your hero

3.2

INSPIRATION

Follow me...

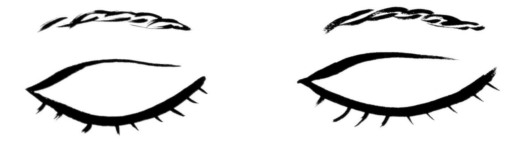

Think of the things
you love the most

Now to **the story**.

Every story must start somewhere, be about
someone – **a character** – and have a plot or an
event that moves the story forward.

The character can have friends or enemies but
most of all, he/she must want something so badly
that it needs to be written down.

Think of a story that you like.

know

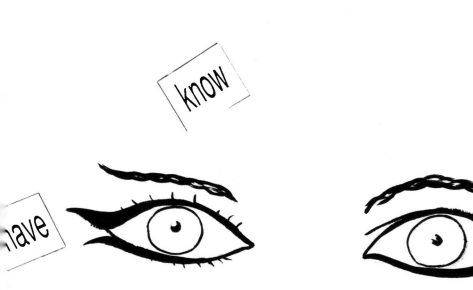

hat

**Are you beginning
to see your story?**

red

dark

whisper

laugh

3.3

THE SEED OF YOUR STORY

Your story will come from two places: inside yourself when you **massage your imagination**, and from **the things you love most in the world**. When you massage your imagination, you'll find all sorts of things that you dream about. And when you think of the things you love most in the world, you'll discover yourself capable of magic. People will do all kinds of impossible things for what they love, even come up with a book. So you too can turn real things into magic and then you will have done something impossible.

Now **write just one sentence** that describes what your story will be about.

You'll be surprised – every story can be summed up in just one sentence. Even the Bible, which is a story as big as the entire universe. So try it.

This single sentence is the **seed of your story**. Scribble it down on a bit of paper, like you would write a secret (ideas often grow in secret), and keep it safe.

Now you have to let your story come out, you have to grow it. Not just what happens, but also how it happens.

The plot

For a story to be a story, something has to happen: things go on as usual until one particular event changes everything. Characters meet, bad things can happen, but so can good things, and this will lead to a certain ending. At the end, the situation is cleared up in some way – it could all end happily, but sometimes also not.

CHARACTERS

The most important person
in your story is the
main character.

Write down everything about him
or her – what are her strong points
and her weak points, what can she do
well? How does she say things? What
does she like? You can even make her an
identity card, with a drawing in the place
of a photo. Your character could even be
an animal – so think about what it is
like, and play with it.
Drawing your character helps. Try
to draw him doing something, or
even better, imagine that he has just
finished doing something and then, at
that instant, dropped down onto the
page. If you think you're not good at
drawing, look at an encyclopaedia and
copy some pictures – all great artists do
that sometimes.

Painting by Marie Charlotte

A story has other characters too – friends or enemies of the main character. Describe all of them.

Your story will come to life with the **moods** that you give it. The way you describe a place and what you turn it into can make even a normal place magical. You also need to put in feelings – love, jealousy, worry, selfishness, fear, loneliness…

Words

The words you use to describe things should be special. They should make the reader see, feel and almost touch everything. They should be able to smell the smells, feel the heat or cold, see the mountains and the rivers. Describe the way your characters talk (sharp voices, high voices, voices as deep as volcanoes), the way one person looks at another, and don't forget the noises things make – trrr, fuffufufu, chrrrr, zazazaza – that's what a world is made of, and that's what you need to create.

So choose each word in your story carefully. And as with the sounds, you can always invent words if you need to – it's your world and you can do anything as long as there's a good reason, and it has to be your reason.

Don't be afraid of making spelling mistakes, what counts is knowing how to tell a story. You can always get help with spelling and grammar later.

Write words for your characters that are funny, serious, happy, sad – just let yourself go and your characters will come to life and seem to walk off the page.

Once you've written something, it's a good idea to read it out loud. It should have a good rhythm, like the tap, tap, tap

FOLLE   MIISTE

of a beat. If there's a word that's making you stumble, get rid of it and write in words that make your story flow like a song.

If you're the silent type or you don't like writing, you could make a book without words, something that moves when you flip through the pages like an animated book, for instance. See *Techniques and Other Muddles* (pg 98).

If, on the other hand, you are crazy about words and you can write beautiful sentences, you could make a feather book – it's made of ribbons and ribbons of paper words. See *Techniques and Other Muddles* (pg 98).

The title

When you give your story a title, it just comes to life.

So spend some time choosing a title – it has to be snappy and indicate what the story is about without giving away the whole plot. It's good if it sounds mysterious.

If you're having a hard time coming up with a title, think of the possibilities, including some that you've heard and like, then choose the best one.

SILENT PERFUME

4 PLANNING YOUR BOOK

Now that you've written your story, it's time to choose the type of book you'd like to make. Choose a book form that suits your particular story and characters. It's great when the form of the book matches the content of the story.

Dividing the story

Read through your story and think of the illustrations that will go along with the words. Now separate the sentences that correspond to an illustration. This is an important step because this will determine the number of pages in your book. When counting the pages of your book, don't forget to include an extra one for your title page.

Mix

4.1

STORYBOARD

Now that you have seen how to divide up your sentences to correspond to the illustrations, think about what you would like your illustrations to be. You will explore this in *Creating Illustrations* (pg 88), but for now quickly draw small sketches of each page of the book. These sketches are called the storyboard.

When creating a storyboard, there are many things to keep in mind:

Technique: what form your book will take, how it will be bound and how the images will be illustrated. (See *Techniques and Other Muddles* pg 98).

Layout and design: what the text and images are going to look like next to each other, and where you're going to place the text and illustrations on a page.

Type: what way you plan to write the text out: in capital letters, normal handwriting, stencilled letters...

Illustrations: your images could be inside a square, rectangle or circle, or take up the whole page. They could be all over the book but there should be reason why they are in a particular place.

Title page: this is the first page where the book's title and the author's name is written.

Cover: this is the part of your book that the world will first see. Don't forget to leave some space for writing your name and the book's title. If your book is thick, it will have a spine – that's the part you see when a book is on a bookshelf.

Taking all these things into account, start making your **storyboard**. Calculate the number of illustrations carefully: these along with your title page will be the total number of pages of your book.

STORYBOARD

4.2

TYPE

The way you write out your story is very important, so make sure you do this carefully. You should take as much care over your handwriting as you would over a drawing. The text can be on the same page as a drawing, on the opposite page, or even inside a picture, if there's a good reason for it. Try making it colourful by writing in one or more colours. You could even write it on top of a splash of colour with a gel pen.

There are lots of fun possibilities:

think of writing in waves

or a spiral   if you're talking of something that's moving,

or in very small writing if it's about secrets,

or Grandly,

like the writing on a royal decree.
How would you write out hiccups?

4.3

COVER

If you remember, I said at the very beginning that a book cover is like a door that lets you into a whole world. Does that make sense now? So your book cover has to invite the reader into the world you've made – it should make people want to immediately open the book and come in. I always make the covers of my books last, but you could start anytime, even when you make your storyboard.

Remember to keep the book neat when it's finished. If a book still has the sticky tape showing or a ragged edge, it doesn't have quite the same power; it doesn't seem quite like a real book. Take some time and effort to put the finishing touches to your book, maybe use some ribbon, or special paper… you'll see the fantastic results of all these little extra efforts you put in.

5 CREATING ILLUSTRATIONS

There are two ways to make a book: you can either draw pictures to a story you write, or write a story to pictures you draw. Here, I'm assuming that you have written your story first and now you need to illustrate it.

You should feel confident drawing pictures to your story. Children make the best paintings without even trying very hard. Every artist would love to be able to draw like you. So feel free, but also be strict with yourself. This means having a good reason for everything you do. Remember, when you draw pictures for a story, it's like the story has got up and started walking around – it actually comes alive!

Drawing by Marie Charlotte

89

5.1

TECHNIQUES

The best technique for illustrations is to mix all the techniques – painting, pencils, crayons and collage – which brings everything together.

The special thing about a **collage** – do you remember our treasure hunt? – is that everything you pick up and use has it's own special nature. But at the same time, you can take what you pick up and turn it into something completely new. So a collage takes bits and pieces, and creates a whole new world. It's a bit like poetry.

Dreams – or even daydreams in which you let yourself be carried away – are like the glue that fixes your collage. You'd be surprised at how your imagination can take you to the strangest places.

Every little thing you pick up can mean any number of things. First you've got to understand what it is, for itself – then let your mind wander along and bring up what it will. For instance, take a cork. A cork floats, right? Just like boats do. So I can make a boat from a piece of cork, and people

who look at that boat think of floating. The boat you make out of cork then becomes more than just a normal boat – it begins to suggest all sorts of meanings.

One warning though: remember not to overdo things, or people will start to get confused about what you mean. It's best to stop with little touches. You need to strike a balance between giving things more meaning and everything getting out of control. Balance is the most important thing for an artist to understand.

5.2

FALLING IN LOVE WITH COLOUR

My friend Marilena is a very good illustrator. When she sees a colour she likes, her mouth begins to water. This doesn't mean you should eat colours – it just means that choosing a colour should be instinctive, something strong inside you. You know the feeling. It's very strong.

Adding colour to an illustration isn't like filling in a colouring book, where you're mainly concentrating on not going over the lines.

Colour is wonderful – it gives shape and light to things, but it also reveals hidden meanings.

A colour can tell you whether the person or thing is happy, sad, worried, dangerous, calm, deep, flat – it's a bit like looking at someone's face and being able to see whether they are happy or sad, worried or calm. You can actually read colour like you can read expressions on a face.

Colour always means something. For instance, say you decide to colour a military tank pink. Of course the pink gives the tank its shape, and maybe makes it shine in the sun, but you've chosen pink, and pink says something about making peace, rather than war. Colour talks.

Colour creates the mood in an illustration. How do you pick up the feeling of a particular place? Through your senses. Colour brings out different feelings. Colour vibrates.

You get a feeling for colour by looking at the world around you, not by looking at your box of paints. Don't you feel a bit down on a dark, cloudy day? And on those crystal clear days when the sky is a pure blue, you feel happy and full of beans, don't you? So your moods have something to do with light, and it's light that makes us see colours. If you look at it another way, it means you can create certain moods by using certain colours.

Colour is a mixture, not just of powder and water and oil and wax and all the things that your paints are made of. Colour carries feelings and thoughts, of places old and far away or new and modern. Or it can simply be ringing inside you like a series of echoes inside a cave.

Magic

Now I'm going to become a magician. But first, let me tell you a little more about colours. Here are the

Primary Colours

Red   *Yellow*   *Blue*

When they combine with each other, they make

Secondary Colours

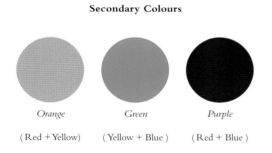

Orange   *Green*   *Purple*

(Red + Yellow)   (Yellow + Blue)   (Red + Blue)

Then there's white:

which makes pink when combined with red.

When added to other colours, white makes them cheerful or sometimes even a bit faded.

I've learned some secrets about colours from my teacher Miguel Fabruccini. One incredible thing he taught me is to mix a touch of white with yellow to make the colour spread better.

And there's black:

which is a bit of a rascal, a bit dangerous. Black makes brown when mixed with red.

When black comes into contact with other colours it makes them look slightly strange – kind of dark and stormy.

And here's a bit of really mysterious magic:

Red and green

Blue and orange

Yellow and purple

These are called **complementary colours**, and they strike up a great friendship. They have no **primary colour** in common and their friendship is so great that if you put red next to green, for instance, the two colours seem much stronger, they boost each other up.

So you see, a colour isn't just lighter or darker or redder or bluer, but it relates to other colours too. Colours have a lot of mystery, and often it's a question of mixing friends together. For instance, when you add a drop of orange to blue, a mysterious reaction takes place and the whole thing becomes a weird grey.

Now I've told you some of my secrets for reading colours and making them. Try combining different colours to make your own magic.

Colours Around You

The best way to get to know colours is to look at them. So find time to lose yourself in the colours around you.

Look at your bedroom, look out of the window at your city, your countryside, the horizon, the wall. Look at the colours in comics, in a film you watch, in a forest, a book, a painting, a piece of furniture, a bowl, a poster, a piece of glass, a box of matches, in somebody's eyes… keep looking, and fall in love with a shy blue or an unusual red, with a cheeky yellow or a dizzy purple.

And don't forget to look at what you would think of as 'non-colours' too. Look for instance at the whiteness on a foggy day that seems to swallow everything up.

It's light and the sun that allow us to see colours. Some colours reflect light, so they're bright, while others keep it quietly closed inside themselves. Keep in mind that a colour can have a shape, it can be transparent or dense. It can change completely when it's put next to another colour. Get used to looking at colours when you're outside, and trying to understand the mixture they're made of.

Look…

95

Soon, it will strike you that colours tell stories.

Take yellow for instance:

 = cheerful yellow

Most times it's cheerful, and sometimes it has a sting. If it's a bit dirty it reminds you of something sick:

= dirty yellow

With a bit of white mixed in it looks happy and playful:

+ ⃝ =

Then with red it turns orange:

 + ● =

And depending on how strongly it's mixed, orange can glow:

 = glowing orange

or become soft like a pumpkin, when there's a little white in it:

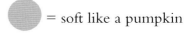 = soft like a pumpkin

Yellow with a drop of green screams springtime:

= *Springtime!*

So colour can impart character: red is fierce, full of action, grand – but with a drop of white, it turns as gentle as a newborn mouse. Blue has lots and lots of possibilities. It can be as cold as ice, as tidy as a uniform, as deep as the sea, and if you put a bit of white and a drop of yellow in it, it becomes as vast and blurry as the sky.

So there are a thousand blues, a thousand pinks, a thousand yellows, a thousand reds, a thousand greens, a thousand blonds, a thousand browns, a thousand whites, a thousand greys, and a thousand blacks. Some colours have incredible names: "running dog" is a light brown, and I've even heard of a colour called "nun's tummy." There's "antique blue," and how many times have I wondered where "ultramarine blue" could carry me?

Over to you...

Test out colours on a piece of paper. It's fun mixing colours, and now you know you have the power to change the character of things, just by adding a drop of colour. It's great to create colours once you've seen a lot of them, and to let yourself be carried away doing it — stir, stir, and you'll see it all come to life.

Remember that if you want a very light colour, start with the white and add your chosen colour little by little.

Try to understand how it all works – how certain colours contrast with others, and how they change when you combine them. Be careful of smearing all the colours into the background when you paint.

Choose the colours that you really love, or those you really hate if you're illustrating a horrible scene. Make friends with colours, and they'll start talking easily about the world you've created.

6 TECHNIQUES & OTHER MUDDLES

Now that you know all these secrets about how to make a book-world, I'll tell you the purely technical secrets and explain how you can construct your books.

Here is a list of things that could be useful – but only to help you organise what you've already got at home. I don't want to make you buy up a whole stationery shop (even though there's nothing I love better) so if there's anything you don't have, use your imagination and do without. The two things that you can't do without are glue and imagination.

- ★ Vinyl glue (Fevicol)
- ★ HB pencil
- ★ Scissors
- ★ Paper cutter
- ★ Clear sticky tape
- ★ Ruler
- ★ Erasers
- ★ Rough string
- ★ Colour pencils
- ★ Watercolours
- ★ Indian ink
- ★ Nibs for calligraphy
- ★ Felt pens that work
- ★ Felt pens that have almost run out
- ★ Pastels
- ★ Oil pastels
- ★ Bright chalks

- ★ Tubes of paint
- ★ Acrylic
- ★ Oil paints (for marbled paper)
- ★ Tracing paper
- ★ Paper fasteners
- ★ Rough, heavy white paper for illustrations (if you don't want to use repainted recycled paper)
- ★ Thick rough paper for covers

6.1

SIMPLE BOOK

Materials

Paper, cardboard, sticky tape, glue, scissors, pencil, ruler

Story and illustrations

1. Write and draw your story on sheets of paper. Make sure all your sheets of paper are the same size and you draw only on one side. Remember to make your title page (where the name of the book and your name appear). Add page numbers to your pages if you like.

2. Lay out your pages in sequence, starting with the title page. Stick each page to the next using sticky tape on the back.

TAPE

3. Attach two sheets of coloured paper (or paper you have decorated yourself), the same size as the rest of your pages, before the title page and after the last page. These are the endsheets.

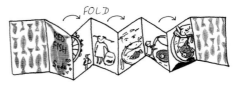

FOLD

Making the book

1. Measure the height and width of your pages.

2. Cut two identical pieces of cardboard, which are 2cm higher and 2cm wider than the size of your pages.

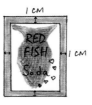

If your pages are 20cm high and 15cm wide, you will have to cut cardboard 22cm high and 17cm wide. One piece will form the front cover and the other the back cover of your book.

3. Now to create the spine of the book. This is the side of the book that you see when it is placed on the shelf. To calculate the thickness of the spine, take your pages and place them one on top of the other and measure the thickness of the pile.

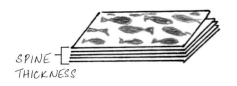

SPINE
THICKNESS

4. Add 10cm to the spine thickness and measure a piece of cardboard for the spine. The height of the spine should be the same as the height of the book covers. Cut out your cardboard for the spine.

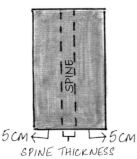

5CM ⟵   ⟶ 5CM
SPINE THICKNESS

5. Measure 5cm from each end of the cardboard for the spine and fold the cardboard to form flaps. This is the spine of your book.

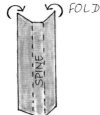

FOLD

6. Now attach the spine cardboard to the front and back cover pieces, by applying glue to the flaps. Wait for it to dry. This is your book cover.

GLUE

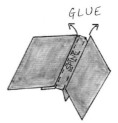

7. Once it is dry, decorate can the cover with any paper you like, glue a nice picture on it, add the title and a whole lot of other decorations.

8. Apply glue to the back of your first endsheet (the one attached to the title page) and stick it onto the inside of your front cover. Glue the second endsheet (the one attached to the last page) to the inside of the back cover.

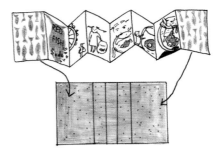

The book is done!

6.2

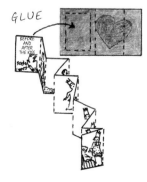

ACCORDION BOOK

Materials

Paper, glue, sticky tape, cardboard, scissors, pencil, ruler, sheet of paper 1 metre long

Story and illustrations

1. For this book, your story and illustrations will be drawn on a strip of paper, about 1 metre long.

1 METRE

2. Decide on the number of pages your book is to have. Divide the long strip of paper into the number of pages you need. Fold your long sheet of paper to form the pages.

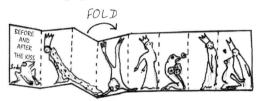

FOLD

3. You can draw your illustrations directly onto the strip of paper or glue

bits onto the pages. You can illustrate on both sides of the paper if you like and you can even do illustrations that spread across two or more pages.
Be sure to leave the back of the title page empty so that you can glue it onto the cover.

Making the book

1. Cut a piece of cardboard that is two and a half times the width of your pages. For example, if each of your pages is 10cm wide, cut your cardboard to 25cm. The height of the cardboard should be 1cm more than the height of the pages.

2. Glue the back of the title page of your book (the one you left empty) to one side of the cover.

GLUE

3. Once the glue is dry, fold the extra part of the cover so that it wraps around the whole book. Your cover will overlap itself.

The book is done!

6.3

NEVER~ENDING BOOK

Materials

Paper, glue, sticky tape, scissors, pencil, ruler

Story and illustrations

Do your illustrations on square pieces of paper. Since this is a never-ending book, write a story that continues without an end, maybe the story of the day in the life of a person or an animal.

Making the book

1. Line up your illustrations, side by side, from first to last. Stick each page to the next using sticky tape on the back.

TAPE

2. This is a book that never ends so you need to join the first page to the last, making a ring of paper – take your strip of illustrations, making sure the illustrations are facing inwards, bring the edges of the first page and the last page together and tape them up.

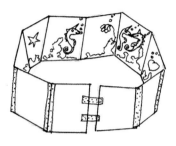

3. Now you have your ring of illustrations, fold them up to form a book.

The book is done!

6.4

THE LEAF BOOK

Materials

Paper, glue, any kind of leaves, string, pin, two big beads

Story and illustrations

1. Your pages are going to be made of leaves for this book, so first dry the leaves you've chosen by putting them inside a notebook, weighed down by a mountain of books.

2. Once the leaves are dry, brush them with diluted colour and glue and allow them to dry again. These are the pages of your book.

3. Do your illustrations on paper, cut them out and glue them onto the leaves, page by page. Don't forget to make a cover by sticking the title, your name and the cover illustration onto one leaf.

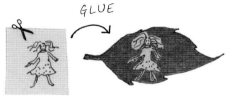

Making the book

1. Take a big bead, thread the string though it and tie two knots to secure it.

2. Order your leaf-pages, starting with the cover. Use a pin to make a hole near the stalk of each leaf. Make sure the holes are the same place on every leaf.

3. Thread the string through the holes in the leaves and pull it tight. Now thread the other bead onto the string and pull it tight so that the beads are holding the the leaves together. Tie up the ends of the string.

The book is done!

6.5

SHAPE BOOK

Materials

Paper, cardboard, sticky tape, glue, scissors, pencil, ruler, coloured ribbon

Story and illustrations

1. The whole book is cut out in a shape, say the shape of the main character or the place where the story is set. For instance, if the main character is a rabbit, cut out all the pages, including the title page, in the shape of a rabbit – just remember to leave an extra flap on the left for binding.

FLAP FOR
BINDING ←

Making the book

1. Put your pages in order, starting with the title page. Put glue on the flaps and stick the pages together. Leave them to dry.

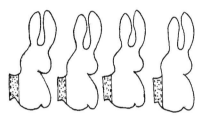

2. To make the cover, trace the outline of your chosen shape on a piece of cardboard. You need two pieces that are mirror images of each other. Remember to leave a little extra space in between for the spine. Cut out your cover.

3. Fold the cover down the centre between the two shapes.

FOLD

4. After the glue on your illustrations has dried, stick the block of illustrations to the cover by gluing the back of the tabs to the cover.

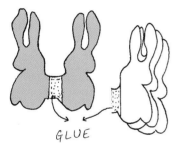

GLUE

The book is done!

6.6

SCROLL BOOK

Materials

Paper, cardboard, sticky tape, glue, paper cutter, scissors, pencil, ruler, compass, sheet of paper 1 metre long, large cardboard tube or sheet of cardboard 23x16cm, long bamboo stick, short bamboo stick.

If you can't get pieces of bamboo, make these sticks yourself: take a sheet of cardboard, roll it up tightly and wrap it with sticky tape so that you have a cardboard stick. For the long stick, use a sheet of cardboard 40x7cm and for the short stick 26x7cm.

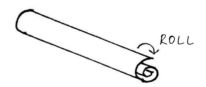

ROLL

Story and illustrations

The whole book is illustrated on a
1 metre strip of paper. Leave 4cm of
space on each end of the paper for the
binding. Draw the title page, followed
by the illustrations and the text, one
after the other.

Making the scroll

1. Take the cardboard tube and cut out
a window measuring 15x3cm, about
4cm from the top of the tube. Or make
a tube, by cutting a piece of cardboard
23x16cm and rolling it to form a tube.
Seal the ends with sticky tape. This is
the body of your scroll.

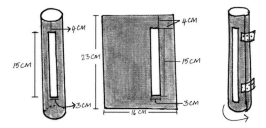

2. Now cut out two cardboard circles,
each of diameter 7cm, from another
piece of cardboard.

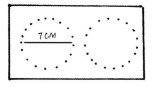

3. Take one of the cardboard circles
and use the compass to draw a circle of
6cm. Draw another circle of 3cm inside
the 6cm circle. Cut out the 3cm circle.

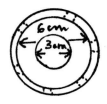

4. Do the same on the other cardboard
circle.

5. With scissors, and starting from the
outside of the 7cm circles, make cut
marks stopping at the 6cm circle. You
will have little flaps around your circles
that you will fold in.

6. Take one of the circles and tape it to
the body of the scroll with sticky tape.

7. Put the long bamboo stick through
the hole in the circle. Tape the other
end of the scroll closed by attaching
the other circle.

8. Cover the scroll completely (except the window) with papier maché (see pg. 60). Make sure to choose some colourful newspaper to cover it with.

Making the book

1. Take the title page end of the long sheet of paper and glue the 4cm empty space that you left at the beginning onto the short bamboo stick. Leave it to dry.

2. Once this is dry, glue the other end of your paper to the long bamboo stick inside the scroll. Leave it to dry.

3. Once it's dry, turn the long bamboo stick until all your illustrations are rolled up inside the scroll.

The book is done!

All you have to do is pull the short bamboo stick and watch your story unfold.

6.7

THE TV BOOK

Materials

Sheet of paper 1 metre long, shoebox or any box with a lid, two bamboo or cardboard sticks, one piece of transparent plastic or wide sticky tape, 1 cork, marbled or handmade paper, glue, sticky tape, paper cutter, scissors, pencil, ruler

If you can't get pieces of bamboo, make these sticks yourself: cut a piece of cardboard 35x7cm, roll it up and wrap it with sticky tape. Strengthen it all over with papier maché (see pg. 60). Make two of these.

ROLL

Making the TV

1. Cut out the TV screen from the box lid, leaving a 5cm edge on three sides and 7cm on the right side.

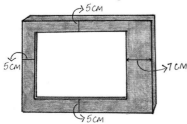

2. Cover the inside of the area you've cut out with a piece of transparent plastic or many strips of wide sticky tape. This is your TV screen.

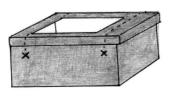

3. Put the lid back onto the box. Measure 1cm down from the edge of the lid and draw a line along the long side of the box. Do the same on the both the long sides of the box.

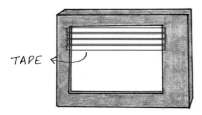

4. Draw a line from the edge of the short side of the screen to intersect with the line you've drawn on the box. Do this on both sides. Mark the points where these lines meet with an X.

5. Cut holes on the box at the four X points, making sure they are the same diameter as your bamboo sticks.

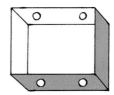

6. Decorate the box and the lid with marbled paper (see pg. 61) or handmade paper.

7. If you want, you can make knobs for the TV using a little slice of cork. (You could even use buttons, or anything else you think would look good as knobs). Stick these next to your screen.

Story and illustrations

1. Once the TV is ready, do your story and illustrations on a long sheet of paper that is 1cm taller than the height of your TV screen.

2. Leave 4cm of space on each end of the paper for the binding.

3. Draw the title page followed by the illustrations, one after the other.

Making the book

1. Starting with the right side of the box, pass one bamboo stick through the holes.

2. Take the paper with your story and attach the 4cm flap at the end of the story to the bamboo stick on the right side of the box. Make sure you wrap and glue the flap firmly around the stick. Leave it to dry.

3. Turn the stick so that your entire story is rolled around it.

4. Take the second bamboo stick and pass it through the holes on the left side of the box.

5. Now stick the flap next to the title page of your story to the second bamboo stick. Leave it to dry.

The book is done!

Turn the left bamboo stick to start your show!

6.8

ANIMATED BOOK

Materials

Thick paper, cardboard, glue, sticky tape, ribbon, scissors, pencil, ruler

Story and illustrations

1. This is a book without words, so there's no written story. It's also called the flip book. As you flick through the pages quickly, you'll see the image moving, almost like in a film. So the seed of the story must be about something that moves — a man waving, a bird flying, a frog jumping, a ball bouncing or a plant growing. The idea is to show the character or object in motion.

2. Cut paper into rectangles of 5x8cm. Mark a margin of 1cm on the left of each page.

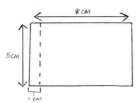

3. Draw the first picture, and then draw the last one. For example, if you're

showing a plant growing, draw the sapling on the first page. Then draw the fully grown plant. Draw the stages of growth on the pages in between, making small changes in each picture until you reach the final stage.

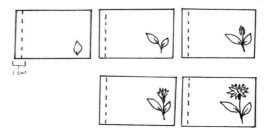

Making the book

1. Place the pages in order, one on top of the other, from first to last. Stick all the pages together putting glue only on the 1cm margin on the left. Leave them to dry. This is your block of illustrations.

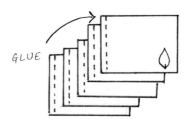

2. Measure the thickness of your block of illustrations. This is the thickness of your spine.

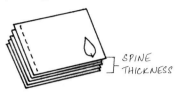

3. Take a piece of cardboard and measure out your cover. The width will be 5cm, the same as your pages. The height will be 16cm + the thickness of the spine.

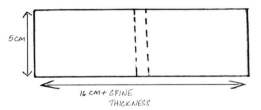

4. Measure 8cm in from the left of the cardboard and draw a line. Do the same from the right of the cardboard. The space in between is the spine. Fold along the lines.

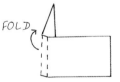

5. Apply glue to the 1cm margin on the back of your block of illustrations. Stick it to the bottom half of the cover. Leave it to dry.

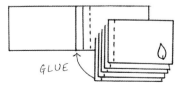

6. Put a finishing touch to the binding by gluing a piece of ribbon over the top margin area. Leave it to dry.

The book is done!

Run your thumb along the edge of the pages to see your character come to life.

6.9

FEATHER BOOK

Materials

Paper, piece of wood or bamboo or anything you can use as a handle, sticky tape, scissors, ribbon, ruler, pencil

Story and illustrations

1. This is a very old type of book, made from lots and lots of strips of paper and looks a bit like a feather duster. Cut strips of paper 20x1.5cm each in lots of different colours.

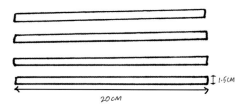

2. Write on them – funny phrases, love notes, instructions, greetings, anything you like.

Making the book

1. Take your piece of wood or bamboo and stick each strip of paper onto the handle with sticky tape. If you can't find bamboo, use a plastic tube or anything that is approximately 10cm long and 3cm in diameter and fits comfortably into your fist.

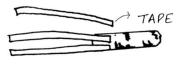

2. Glue a colourful ribbon around the base to hide the sticky tape.

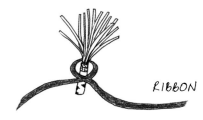

The book is done!

Now you can rustle your wise words in someone's face.

6.10

POP~UP BOOK

Materials

Thick paper, sticky tape, scissors, paper cutter, ruler, glue

Story and illustrations

Think up a story with surprises and with characters that move to make a pop-up book. And here are some tricks to make things in your book move…

To make a door open

1. Draw a door on a sheet of paper and cut it out, leaving and extra 1cm on the left.

2. On the page of your book, use a paper cutter to make a slit where the door hinge should be. Make sure the slit is the same height as your door.

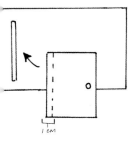

FRONT

1 CM

3. Push the 1cm tab through the slit, turn the page over and glue the tab onto the back.

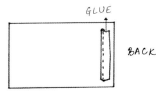

GLUE

BACK

4. Open the door and say 'Hello' to your character.

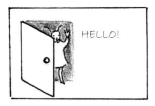

HELLO!

To make characters move

1. Draw your character with one of its arms ending at the elbow. On another piece of paper, draw the forearm (from the elbow to the hand) and cut it out.

2. Place the cut-out forearm onto the illustration, matching elbow to elbow. Make a little hole in the middle of the elbow and put a paper fastener into it. Turn the illustration over and open out the pins of the paper fastener.

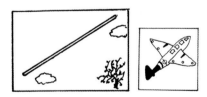

3. You can use this technique to make many other body parts move.

To make a plane fly

1. Make a slit across your page with a paper cutter. The slit should be as long as the path your plane will fly in the sky. Draw a plane on another piece of paper and cut it out.

2. Take a strip of thick paper and make a small fold at the end. Glue your plane onto the folded part.

3. Push the paper strip through the slit on your page, leaving the plane in front.

4. Move the strip behind the page and watch your plane fly.

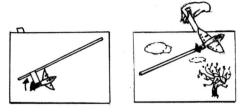

Making a frog jump

1. Draw a pond on your page. Draw the frog on a separate piece of paper and cut it out.

2. Cut a strip of paper 5cm wide and 1cm high. Fold the paper zig-zag like a spring.

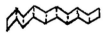

3. Glue one end of the spring on the back of the frog. Leave it to dry.

GLUE

4. Once it is dry, stick the other end of the spring on the pond on your page. Leave it to dry. Your frog is all set to jump.

Making the book

Gather all your pages together and follow the cover and binding techniques of the simple book (see pg. 100) to create your pop-up book.

6.11

BOOK~IN~THREE

Materials

Paper for illustrations, thick paper or cardboard for cover, sticky tape, scissors, paper cutter, ruler

Story and illustrations

1. Each page of this playful book is divided into three parts. It has no story but it can be very funny. Match different heads with different bodies and legs to make strange characters.

2. Cut paper 18cm high and 11cm wide. Mark a 1cm margin on the left of each page for the binding.

3. On each page, measure 6cm down from the top and draw a line from the margin to the edge of the page.

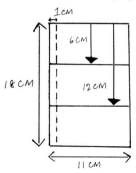

4. Take the pages, measure 12cm down from the top and draw another line.

5. Now draw your illustrations. Make sure the face is on the top section, the body on the middle section and the legs on the lower section. Do all your illustrations this way.

6. Once your illustrations are done, use scissors to cut the pages along the 6cm and 12 cm lines, stopping at the margin. All your pages will now be in three parts, held together by the margin.

7. Draw your title pages separately on a piece of paper without any cuts. Remember to leave the 1cm margin on the left for the binding.

Making the book

1. Starting with the title page, gather all the pages and put glue on the 1cm margin on the left and stick them together. Dry.

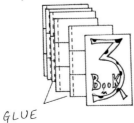

GLUE

2. Measure your block of pages to find the thickness of the spine.

SPINE
THICKNESS

3. For the cover, cut thick paper or cardboard to these measurements: height 18.5cm and width 22cm + spine thickness.

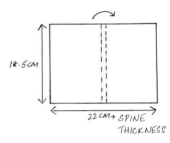

18.5CM

22 CM + SPINE
THICKNESS

4. Fold the cover around the block of pages and crease the spine area.

5. Stick the margin area of the pages to the spine with glue.

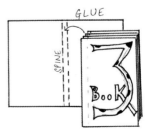

GLUE

SPINE

6. Finish the spine by sticking on a pretty ribbon or some fabric.

The book is done!

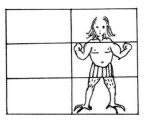

Now go ahead and mix and match heads, bodies and legs. See what strange characters you can create, maybe a girl with the body of a wrestler and the legs of a chicken and many, many more.

7

WORKSHOPS

I love having participants of different ages in my bookmaking workshops, anyone from 5 to 14 years old. The smaller ones are bursting with ideas and get the older ones to help them with writing, and when the older ones lack inspiration they ask the little ones for advice, and it always works well.

A gift from India

The workshop that is documented here took place in Chianti (Tuscany, Italy) in a mill that was lent to us for the occasion by Luca and Raphaelle Benini. There were six children and three adults (the photographer Giulio Pietromarchi, Eleonora Sgaravatti and myself).

The most exciting thing about the workshop was that the material we were to use was from India. We had planned the workshop for months, with children coming from Rome, Todi and Paris.

We had been waiting for ages for this box from India to arrive. Gita Wolf and Sirish Rao

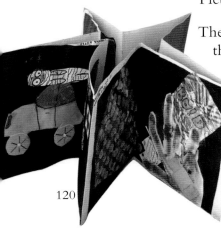

Infinite book by Maurizio

from Tara Publishing were to send us this Pandora's box, and we knew it would be extraordinary. So we waited and waited and waited…

It was already the day before the workshop and the first child arrived, then the second, the third, the fourth, the fifth, and the last was picked up from the airport… but the box still wasn't there.

Then came a text message from Rome: "The box has arrived."

And when it came to us in the August heat (44 degrees in the shade), we all went to receive it at the station and ran home with it. We stood around the open box — I don't think I've ever been so thrilled in my life.

Gita and Sirish had chosen the things with such care: cloth, all kinds of paper, ribbons, wire, beads, mirrors, newspapers, kitschy magazines of all sorts, old posters, strips of paper, test pages from the screen-printing of their books… it was a treasure chest! As I pulled things out of it, I heard cries of excitement all around me, and the children started taking the things they liked best, all ready to start work the next day.

The following pages show the work that the children came up with, over the course of the workshop.

As for the box, I'll always keep it in my study, it's the richest and most useful gift I've ever received.

Leaf book by Marie Charlotte

ANTILLA age 10

SCROLL BOOK

Materials

Glue, brushes, pencil, felt pens, pastels, bamboo pieces and leaves, scissors, Indian newspapers, recycled paper, tube from kitchen towel, little mirrors, pieces of Indian material, foil

Massaging your imagination

your favourite word: **Antilla** · the word you hate most: **Cyanide** · a word you don't understand: **Sherlock** · a grown-up's word: **Work** · a scary word: **Murderer** · a word that makes you feel sleepy: **Tse tse** · a word that makes you dream: **Italy** · a magic word: **Open parsley** · a hypnotic word: **Mischief** · everything you wish for in three words: **Warmth, water, friendship** · a weapon-word: **Violence** · a kind word: **Thank you** · a historic word: **Humanity** · a word that sounds funny: **Marbou**

or beezlebub · an animal: **Puma** · a gift: **Friendship** · a friend: **Matilde** · a magic potion: **Courgettes, vinegar, ostrich thigh, banana skin and cloves, Amazonian onion and pink grapefruit juice** · a bizarre plant: **Cactus** · your suitcase: **A book, my toothbrush, a skirt, some trousers, a t-shirt, a watch, my underwear and a pair of sandals** · a metamorphosis: **Caterpillar, butterfly** · your imaginary country: **Silly-land** · describe your forest: **A forest of palms and banana trees** · a journey: **Venezuela: The Orinoco** · a secret code: **AFX6407SP** · your favourite colour: **Yellow** · your favourite number: **3** · a trap: **Look-alike** · an obstacle: **Wall** · someone who helps you: **The brain** · a maze: **The jungle** · a refuge: **My house** · your favourite prince: **Daddy** · your favourite princess: **Catherine of Monaco** · your house: **Tropical shack** · your hero: **Me**

The story

This story started one afternoon when a camel called Mel and his mother went for a walk. Suddenly, Mel walked away from his mother to go and drink from the river. He turned round and he couldn't see his mother anywhere, so he called out, but nobody answered. He tried again, but again nobody answered. After a while he gave up, and, sobbing, he went back to their house in the jungle.

On the way he met a marabou who asked him, "Why are you crying?"
"I've lost my mum."
The next morning he went back to the river and on the way he saw the marabou again, who asked him "Have you seen your mother?"
"No, not yet."
"If you want, I can help you."
"Thanks."
So the marabou grasped the camel's hump and flew off with him. They landed to meet the marabou's friend, the monkey.
So Mel asked the monkey, who was looking at herself in the mirror, "Excuse me but I don't suppose you've seen a female camel?"
"Is this her?" she asked, pointing to the mirror.
"Yes, thanks so much," he said, running towards his mother.
From that day on, the camel and the marabou became friends.

MAURIZIO age 13

FABRIC SHOP SHAPE BOOK

Materials

Wrapping paper, cardboard, rough paper, pastels, old felt pens (for a faded effect), pencils, fountain pen, shiny glue, an Indian button, fabric, bamboo, sticky tape

Massaging your imagination

your favourite word: **Life** · the word you hate most: **War** · a word you don't understand: **War** · a grown-up's word: **Tax** · a scary word: **War** · a word that makes you feel sleepy: **Conference** · a word that makes you dream: **Rome** · a magic word: **Abracadabra** · a hypnotic word: **Money** · Everything you wish for in three words: **Happiness, life, luck** · a weapon-word: **Blackmail** · a kind word: **Thank you** · A historic word: **Revolution** · a word that sounds funny: **Exuberant** · an animal: **Cheetah** · a

gift: **Friendship** · a friend: **Matteo** ·
a magic potion: **Water, moose broth,
paracetamol, trout's eggs, couscous,
put it all in a saucepan with some oil
and fry for two minutes, put it in the
freezer and you'll get a very good
ice cream** · a bizarre plant: **Ivy** · your
suitcase: **Toothbrush, t-shirt, desire for
adventure, camera** · a metamorphosis:
Antilla, little toad · your imaginary
country: **Italy** · describe your forest:
Uncontaminated greenery · a journey:
Round the world · your favourite
colour: **Blue** · your favourite number:
3 · A trap: **Swindle** · an obstacle:
Door · someone who helps you: **A
pen** · a maze: **Rome** · a refuge: **My
room** · your favourite prince: **Me** ·
your favourite princess: **Diana** · your
house: **His address** · your castle: **Club
chichoto** · your hero: **Me**

The story

Once upon a time there was a young
tailor in Calcutta who earned so little
from his job that he had just enough to
survive.

One day an old lady came into his shop
to buy an overcoat to cover up her
scrawny little body. Unfortunately she
didn't have enough money for it. So
the compassionate young tailor Babul
gave the coat to the old lady for free.
At this point, the old lady disappeared
under the coat and a young Indian girl
dressed like a princess from the olden
days appeared. "Hello, my name is
Siritha. Thank you for the coat. You are
just the kind of person I was looking
for. Keep this, it will help you on the
mission you are going to have to do,
it's magic," said the princess to Babul,
holding out a roll of blue material, and
without giving him time to reply she
continued, "You have to go the palace
of the Sultan of Bagathar to free my
father Sithar, good luck!" And without
giving the poor tailor time to answer,
she vanished leaving behind the coat
and a bag of gold coins.

The young man stood there open-
mouthed, staring at the spot from
which young Siritha had vanished,
for at least 10 minutes. Then all of a
sudden he took the roll of material and
the bag of coins, closed the door to the
shop and ran as fast as his feet would
carry him to Bagathar. He ran for two
days and finally arrived in front of the
Sultan's palace and fell to the ground
exhausted.

When he woke up, he was in a garden
with an old man who said, "Poor
young man, you've been condemned
to death just because you fell asleep
in front of the Sultan's palace and we
can't escape – no, because there's a tiger
guarding the exit."

"I've got an idea," said Babul, and he
started sewing a blue tiger from the roll
of material.

When the tiger was ready, it attacked
the other tiger, and the two men
escaped. All of a sudden the tiger
turned into Siritha who hugged Babul
and then the old man, who was her

father. Two months later the whole of Calcutta celebrated the wedding of Babul the tailor with Siritha.

Maurizio also made an...

INFINITE BOOK

Materials

Old printed pages that had black parts on them, white gel pen, yellow sticky tape, wood-effect paper, holographic paper, wrapping paper, tin foil, felt pens, plasters, a beauty spot, glitter, polka-dotted plastic, magazines, masking tape, glue

The story

The woodworm is playing on his Playstation. His mother, who is furious, turns off the TV and sends him to do some work. But after a while the woodworm gets tired of digging tunnels and goes for a walk. The lady of the house sprays him with anti-woodworm spray. He ends up in intensive care at Saint Woodworm's hospital. And then he goes home, goes back to playing on his Playstation... and the story starts again.

NICOLA age 10

SIMPLE BOOK

Materials

Masking tape, shiny tape, shiny glue, gold and silver glitter glue, felt pens, a capital letter in relief, coloured thread, pastels, pencil, gold pen, an Indian button, fuzzy sticker, gold chain, prints from books, party decorations, scraps of Indian magazines

Massaging your imagination

your favourite word: **Maybe "dunno"**
• the word you hate most: **Grammar**
• a word you don't understand: **Car**
• a grown-up's word: **Work** • a scary word: **Ripper** • a word that makes you feel sleepy: **Talking too much** • a word that makes you dream: **Multi-coloured** • a magic word: **Signs** • a hypnotic word: **Turn, turn, turn** • Everything you wish for in three words: **Sea,**

125

friendship, happiness · a weapon-word: **Bazooka** · a kind word: **Good day** · a historic word: **Renaissance** · a word that sounds funny: **Hitler** · an animal: **Tiger** · a gift: **Beyblade** · a friend: **Tano** · a magic potion: **Bluebeard's hairs, blended lizard, shark's jaw, chopped snakes' tails, frogs' feet, put it all in a cauldron, blend it all together and cook for 24 hours** · a bizarre plant: **Carnivorous plant** · your suitcase: **Clothes, toys and shoes** · a metamorphosis: **Wolf man** · your imaginary country: **Full of nature, everything free and you know everybody** · describe your forest: **A very thick forest with wooden huts with smoke coming out of the chimneys** · a journey: **To Sardinia** · a secret code: **3 16 93 X** · your favourite colour: **Green and blue** · your favourite number: **3** · a trap: **A very taut wire and when you trip over it, a one ton weight falls on your head** · an obstacle: **Circles of fire** · someone who helps you: **Maurizio** · a maze: **At the market full of people** · a refuge: **In the hideout of the chichotos** · your favourite prince: **The Little Prince** · your favourite princess: **Sleeping Beauty** · your house: **His address** · your castle: **Hermitage** · your hero: **Samurai Jack**

The story
The Adventure of the Magnificent Bird

Once upon a time there was a magnificent bird. The bird was flying south for winter but was hit by a bullet. He sank into the sea and was sucked into an underwater black hole. When he woke up, the Chameleon King said to him, "Well, you're just the person we were looking for for the National Competition of Lost Mazes."
The bird said, "But I don't want to take part."
"In that case we'll have to use torture instruments on you."
So the bird accepted. Three days later, the big day arrived.
"Our champion JACK the Chameleon against the Foreign Magic Bird."
And everyone laughed: AHAHAHAHAHAHAHA!!!!"
"Now the first clue is: under the statue of Leonardo d'Avinci there's a secret passage under the floor."
"The first point is won by JACK," said the presenter. "The second clue is: they're rings but you can't put them on your fingers or you'll get burnt."
The bird was passing through the fifth and final ring but the chameleon stuck out his tongue and moved the last ring. So the presenter said, "Sorry Magic Bird, but this point goes to nobody." So the bird thought, "You really are a Bip of a Bip!"
The third clue was: "If you want to go into a lock in a door, you have to

look." The chameleon opened the door and made a potion. This potion had to be drunk by the tiger who was meant to spit it at the carnivorous plant, and in this way the door of the maze would open.

But the chameleon was eaten by the tiger. So the bird took his potion and made the tiger drink it. The tiger spat it at the carnivorous plant which turned into the exit to the maze. They gave the bird the trophy and he was able to go back to his own world.

MARIE CHARLOTTE

age 10

SIMPLE BOOK

Materials

Pastels, felt pens, sequins, pieces of adverts, fig leaves, spaghetti, recycled paper, Indian newspapers, tracing paper, brushes

Massaging your imagination

your favourite word: **Flowery** · the word you hate most: **Filthy** · a word you don't understand: **Consequences** · a scary word: **Skull** · a word that makes you feel sleepy: **Talking too much** · a word that makes you dream: **A carrot hanging from a thread** · a magic word: **Thank you** · a hypnotic word: **Bird** ·

Everything you wish for in three words: **A red horse** · a weapon-word: **Sword** · a kind word: **I adore** · a historic word: **To love** · a word that sounds funny: **Moishe** · an animal: **Beaver** · a gift: **Some springs** · a friend: **A whale** · a magic potion: **A syrup** · a bizarre plant: **Cactus** · your suitcase: **Full of cotton and clothes** · describe your forest: **Trees, trousers that walk by themselves and talking flowers** · a journey: **America** · a secret code: **AB49** · your favourite colour: **Pink** · your favourite number: **16** · a trap: **A trap** · someone who helps you: **Mummy** · a maze: **A forest** · a refuge: **A horrible house** · your favourite prince: **The Mute Prince** · your favourite princess: **The Princess of Strawberries** · your house: **A house in the countryside** · your castle: **Medieval castle** · your hero: **The Mute Prince**

The story

Princess Chloe Gets Married

One day a girl is walking down the street with her arms full of groceries, and she drops them all. A young man helps her pick up her groceries and they start exchanging romantic glances – it's love at first sight.

The young man invites Chloe out to dinner at a restaurant with his parents and Chloe, who is head over heels in love, accepts.

The years go by until one day the young man asks Chloe to marry him. She accepts and then adds, "All right, but you have to be a prince."

"Ok, if that's what you want but I'll marry you anyway, so let's get married tomorrow."

The next day the princess got up at seven o'clock in the morning to get ready. When everybody arrived, they saw that the bride was the most beautiful ever and everyone fainted, and the photographers' films were used up in ten seconds.

All this is to tell you that a splendid bride will always find herself alone with her husband!

TANO age 10
RUBY-SHAPED BOOK

Materials

Red glitter, silver and gold shiny glue, coloured thread, little Indian mirrors, Indian newspaper, Indian buttons, printed paper, tin foil, wood-effect paper, crayons, shimmering coloured sticky tape, shiny paper, felt pens, pencil, Indian stickers

Massaging your imagination

your favourite word: **Superspeedy** · the word you hate most: **Bush, homework, Daniel** · a word you don't understand: **Homogenized** · grown-up's word: **Engineering** · a scary word: **Gloomy** · a word that makes you feel sleepy: **Good night** · a word that makes you dream: **World** · a magic word: **Simsala bim** · a hypnotic word: **Yoyo** · everything you wish for in three words: **Friendship, PlayStation, holiday** · a weapon-word: **Rocket launcher** · a kind word: **Thank you** · a historic word: **Neolithic** · a word that sounds funny: **Macarena** · an animal: **Berlusconi** · a gift: **Jak 2** · a friend: **Nicola** · a magic potion: **Rib of Berlusconi, eyes of Bush, moustache of Hitler, beard of Bin Laden and Saddam** · a bizarre plant: **Ivy** · your suitcase: **Shoes, t-shirt, trousers** · a metamorphosis: **Caterpillar, chrysalis, butterfly** · your imaginary country: **Just friendliness** · describe your forest: **A forest full of colour and lots of animals** · a journey: **To America** · a secret code: **12/16/93 TFM** · your favourite colour: **Gold** · your favourite number: **16** · a trap: **Make a hole and cover it with leaves** · an obstacle: **Circles of fire** · someone who helps you: **My brother** · a maze: **Full of fire that follows you around** · a refuge: **In the house of the chichotos** · your favourite prince: **Prince Charming** · your favourite princess: **Snow White** · your house: **Small but beautiful** · your castle: **Very big with lots of secret passages** · your hero: **Rambo**

The story

Once upon a time there was a thief who wanted to steal the Ruby of Goodness.

One day he went to the museum and stole it. And everybody became mean, except the museum guards.

He escaped and ran to forest. The guards tried to follow him but they lost sight of him. He hid in a cave where there was a very strange little animal.

Then the guards found him and recovered the Ruby, but they didn't notice the animal who, without being seen, followed the thief and freed him and people became kind again and lived happily ever after.

MATILDE age 5
FEATHER BOOK
Materials

Bamboo, masking tape, sticky tape, strips of printed paper, felt pens

Massaging your imagination

your favourite word: **Princess** · the word you hate most: **Pig** · a word you don't understand: **Oleander** · a grown-up's word: **Rifle** · a scary word: **Lioness** · a word that makes you feel sleepy: **Lullaby** · a word that makes you dream: **Prince** · a magic word: **Magician** · a hypnotic word: **Tree** · everything you wish for in three words: **Prince**

Charming, Bratz dolls and flowers ·
a weapon-word: **Sword** · a kind word:
Window · a historic word: **You** · a
word that sounds funny: **Thunder** ·
an animal: **Monkey** · a gift: **Barbie** ·
a friend: **Giuseppe and Francesca** · a
magic potion: **Pear, orange, banana,
snakeskin and tail, frog soup** · a
bizarre plant: **Bamboo** · your suitcase:
**Dolls, clothes, talking bed, plant,
son** · a metamorphosis: **Snake** · your
imaginary country: **Florence** · describe
your forest: **The wolf's forest with
a scary drawing and a witch** · a
journey: **To Florence on horseback** · a
secret code: **Padlock** · your favourite
colour: **All of them** · your favourite
number: **0** · a trap: **The police in
Rome** · an obstacle: **A tree** · someone
who helps you: **My brother** · a maze:
Full of fire that follows you around
· a refuge: **Mummy in bed** · your
favourite prince: **Prince Charming**
· your favourite princess: **Princess
Fiona** · your house: **Beautiful** · your
castle: **It's in Rome** · your hero: **Prince
Charming**

Thank you

Giulio Pietromarchi for the photographs
and for his talent,
Luca and Raphaelle Benini for the Mill in
which the workshops took place,
Carlo Alvarez de Castro, Sita A. Banerjee,
Emanuela Benini, Tomaso Botti, Giovanna
Calvino, Marie Charlotte Daudenet, Katya
Falla Alvarez de Castro,
Maurizio Fürst, Antilla Fürst, Christine
Khondji, Darius Khondji, Benedetto
Pietromarchi, Matilde Pietromarchi,
Nicola Pietromarchi, Tano Risi, Petroc
Sesti, Eleonora Sgaravatti, Anna Spadolini
e Guido Lagomarsino.
Miguel Fabruccini for the genial openness
of his teaching.
Thank you to everyone who lets me
daydream.

The Book Book: A Journey into Bookmaking
First published in English by Tara Books, 2007
Copyright © 2007
Second Printing 2009

For the text and illustrations:
Sophie Benini Pietromarchi

For this edition:
Tara Publishing Ltd., UK <www.tarabooks.com/uk>
and
Tara Books, India <www.tarabooks.com>

Printed in China by Leo Paper Products Limited

ISBN: 978-81-86211-24-3